WE HUMANS ARE BLESSED

PRANJAL BORKAR

Contents

1. A Big Thankyou 1

2. Meaning Of Life 10

3. Be Happy 21

4. Humanity For Humans 32

5. What Matters? 45

6. Experience Teach Us 55

7. Birth To Death 66

8. Some Are Good ,some Are Bad 71

9. Hurdles We Need To Come Across 81

10. Life Defines 86

11. Be Hero Of Your Life 91

12. Achieve Your Goals 98

13. Stories 109

1
A Big Thankyou

Thankyou god

I thank god for each and every thing he gave me everything . Eyes he gave to see this wonderful world , Ears to hear ,Nose to smell ,Tongue to test and Skin to sense . Not only all this but also most precious gift he gave is parents . nothing more a person wants in his or her life instead of there five sense organs and their parents with them nothing more a person wanted in their lives. We should be thankfull to god that he gave each and every necessity to fullfill our life with red roses . we preach to god when we find ourselves in difficulties and we try to overcome through that situation being a person we all are somewhere selfish we live for our own sake of happiness all that we want is that we mean to is our own happiness so when we find ourselves in trouble we will go to god we will preach them for our own sake of happiness and success when we are happy that time we even don't go to temple or even we don't see him all that we see that time is just we are happy so there is no need to preach to god but peoples are unaware about it that today if we are happy the reason of our happiness is god . when we are in trouble we get worried and come through anxiety and we fear so when we have that one mindset in our self belief is that nothing is going to happen god is with us he will o all things fine . That time we calm ourselves by saying this time also be passed . Something we should thank god is for the reason of giving this exciting and overwhelming life always it will be not the situation with anyone that we will be always sad or always happy because if we are happy it doesn't mean that we will never be sad again in life .many of us don't believe in god as they think that as you sow , you reap yea its absolutely right but this all is what our karma tells us that means that how you are sustaining yourself in society , society will give this back to you as it will not be the condition that if you are behaving with all peoples rudely and they will be kind towards you . if your attitude is ruddy towards them obviously, they will be same towards you . here I would mention one thing that god is a power of peace, honesty , politeness ,patience, bravery. Now if god gave such a miserable life to us should we live this life with full of stress and fear or should we enjoy it yes we should enjoy our life we should live our life hurdles are key to surpass in our life I agree that we are the people who always be stressed of our jobs and our daily routine and we run behind success in our life trying to achieve success is good but only hardworking and being stressed cant help out all that is we should live our life , we should over come each and every situation with a big smile on our face . our smile is the best weapon to kill our enemies . being patient and kind will help us to come to a situation where we will be at the top of the world even if we work hard and we achieve success this will be happiness for us for may be one day, one week or one year but if you enjoy each and every second of your life it will you happiness which will be endless and absolutely what we want is in our life is being calm and fearless. "once you become fearless your life becomes limitless". So now all that is we need to decide do we want a happy and endless life or an stressful and anxious life. So the best medicine to kill the disease stress and fear is being happy and calm. As per the research it has been proved that meditation is the best way to calm ourself and keep our body and soul together. Being the one for others happiness is something more than being the reason for others sadness . you tease others , make them fear , etc... but ever it happened that ever you be the reason of others smile if not then you should be . Anyone can be sad in sad situation but being happy in sad situation is something more . being the one to be a fighter and warrior will make you amaze and your astonishing way of fighting to your problems will rise you above your goals and ambition through each circumstances of life .

You can be a warrior, happier, success personality, honest , calm, patient, witty, clever, genius , extraordinary, marvellous, fantastic , unique you will be all this but if you will preach god in every way of your life if you share your each happy and sad day with him he will definitely make you calm.

There are many lives on our earth . we all humans have right to do everything we are only the life on earth who are considered as most intelligent lives as we have most precious thing withus that is nothing but our brain .

I wondered that whats the meaning of life? I came to the conclusion that what really matters is the more that we can increase scope and skill of human consciousness, the better we are able to ask this questions. Our life can be just about solving problems otherwise whats the point. We are multi-planet species and scope and scales of consciousness is expanded across many civilizationsand many planets and many star future it is a wonderful thing to me.

I would like to share a story here there was a man who sat with his son near a bridge , there the boy asks his father that what is the value of my life there his father gives him a stone and he says him that go to the market don't speak anything and just the thing is this stone has to be sold by you and whenever person ask the price of the stone just show your two fingers . the boy goes to market a lady asks the boy what is the price of the stone he shows his two fingers then the lady gives him 2 dollar , he comes to home and he says to his father that a lady gave me 2 dollar for that stone . his father gives him another stone and says him to go to a museum and to sell it but whenever any person asks the price just show your two fingers he goes to the meuseum and there a man from that museum asks him what is the price of this stone the boy shows his 2 fingers and the man gives him 200 dollar then after that he comes home and the his father tells him to go to shop of precious stones and there if anyone ask what is price of stone show your 2 fingers then the boy goes the person from precious stones shop asks to him what is the price of stone? He shows to fingers and man gives him 200,000 dollar he was elated and comes home .his father said to him then life is all about where you place it.

"It does not matter how long you are spending on the earth, how much money you have

gathered or how much attention you have received. It is the amount of positive vibration you have radiated in life that matters,"

when we look back on our life ....in our last breaths... we will all wonder...

did my life mean anything? did my life mean anything to this world?did i have impact on anyone else 's life...Did i matter?

we wont be worried about our bills, we wont be worried about our hair ,we certainly wont care about our favourite t.v. show... we wont spare a second thought of other opinions and judements... before you reach the last breath today might be the time to make change... MAKE YOUR LIFE MATTER! There will be two dates either side of dash , make sure that dash is not empty . make sure that it is full of life. FULL of living.

Oscar Wilde once said "To live is the rarest thing in the world. Most people exist , that is all." and we was write dont live like everyone else... EXISTING... BE EXTRAORIDINARY, LIVE EVERY MOMENT WITH PASSION AND WONDER. Dont take ANYTHING OR ANYONE FOR GRANTED! What is important *to you? , What dreams do you have? GO GET THEM! What are you waiting for ?*

DO ALL THINGS RIGHT NOW YOU NEVER KNEW IT WILL BE YOUR LAST CHANCE. Dont take this magical thing called life for granted.... "KEEP YOUR HEAD WHEN EVERYONE ELSE IS LOSING THEIRS" " TRUST YOURSELF WHEN EVERYONE DOUBTS YOU" " MASTER YOUR DREAMS WHEN ALL OTHERS GIVE UP ON THEIRS " "BE THE CAPTAIN WHEN EVERYONE ELSE IS CONTENT BEING THE CREW" "BE THE LION WHEN ALL OTHERS ARE PLAYING SHEEPS" "BE THE LEADER WHEN ALL OTHERS ARE FOLLOWING" Live each day as if it may be your last day on EARTH " LIVE YOUR LEGACY"

HUMAN LIFE life is the most precious God gift to every one whether it is human, bird, animal or plant it does not matter. But human life is more important than others. it has includes plenty and wide meanings in itself. it is not only about breathing. If the human do only breathing, eating and reproduction then there will be no difference between human and other living beings.
Nowadays I am seeing that human life is going worst than others. humans are becoming selfish. They think only about their personal

benefits not for others. life on earth is possible just because of nature. nature teaches us that life is all about giving to others. Life is a debt on you by nature, parents, society. Human have to give back whatever he get before birth to till die. Rivers give their water to us. Trees give their fruits to...show more content...

1. Do not take rest after your first victory because if you fail in second, more lips are waiting to say that your first victory was just luck.

2. All birds find shelter during a rain. But eagle avoids rain by flying above the clouds.

3. Failure will never overtake me if my definition to succeed is strong enough.

4. Man needs difficulties in life because they are necessary to enjoy the success.

5. If you want to shine like a sun. First burn like a sun.

6. It is very easy to defeat someone, but it is very hard to win someone.

7. All of us do not have equal talent, but all of us have an equal opportunity to develop our talents.

Awesome
Quotes
Dear God,
Thank you for
everything

2
Meaning of life

Life is a characteristic that distinguishes physical entities that have biological processes, such as signaling and self-sustaining processes, from those that do not, either because such functions have ceased (they have died), or because they never had such functions and are classified as inanimate. Various forms of life exist, such as plants, animals, fungi, protists, archaea, and bacteria. Biology is the science concerned with the study of life. There is currently no consensus regarding the definition of life. One popular definition is that organisms are open systems that maintain homeostasis, are composed of cells, have a life cycle, undergo metabolism, can grow, adapt to their environment, respond to stimuli, reproduce and evolve. Other definitions sometimes include non-cellular life such viruses and viroids. Abiogenesis is the natural process of life arising from non-living matter, such as simple organic compounds. The prevailing scientific hypothesis is that the transition from non-living to living entities was not a single event, but a gradual process of increasing complexity. Life on Earth first appeared as early as 4.28 billion years ago, soon after ocean formation 4.41 billion years ago, and not long after the formation of the Earth 4.54 billion years ago. The earliest known life forms are microfossils of bacteria. Researchers generally think that current life on Earth descends from an RNA world, although RNA-based life may not have been the first life to have existed. The classic 1952 Miller–Urey experiment and similar research demonstrated that most amino acids, the chemical constituents of the proteins us

in all living organisms, can be synthesized from inorganic compounds under conditions intended to replicate those of the early Earth. Complex organic molecules occur in the Solar System and in interstellar space, and these molecules may have provided starting material for the development of life on Earth.Since its primordial beginnings, life on Earth has changed its environment on a geologic time scale, but it has also adapted to survive in most ecosystems and conditions. Some microorganisms, called extremophiles, thrive in physically or geochemically extreme environments that are detrimental to most other life on Earth. The cell is considered the structural and functional unit of life. There are two kinds of cells, prokaryotic and eukaryotic, both of which consist of cytoplasm enclosed within a membrane and contain many biomolecules such as proteins and nucleic acids. Cells reproduce through a process of cell division, in which the parent cell divides into two or more daughter cells. In the past, there have been many attempts to define what is meant by "life" through obsolete concepts such as odic force, hylomorphism, spontaneous generation and vitalism, that have now been disproved by biological discoveries. Aristotle was the first person to classify organisms. Later, Carl Linnaeus introduced his system of binomial nomenclature for the classification of species. Eventually new groups and categories of life were discovered, such as cells and microorganisms, forcing dramatic revisions of the structure of relationships between living organisms. Though currently only known on Earth, life need not be restricted to it, and many scientists speculate in the existence of extraterrestrial life. Artificial life is a computer simulation or human-made reconstruction of any aspect of life, which is often used to examine systems related to natural life. Death is the permanent termination of all biological functions which sustain an organism, and as such, is the end of its life. Extinction is the term describing the dying out of a group or taxon, usually a species. Fossils are the preserved remains or traces of organisms.

The question of the meaning of life is perhaps one that we would rather not ask, for fear of the answer or lack thereof.

Still today, many people believe that we, humankind, are the creation of a supernatural entity called God, that God had an intelligent purpose in creating us, and that this intelligent purpose is "the meaning of life".

I do not propose to rehearse the well-worn arguments for and against the existence of God, and still less to take a side. But even if God exists, and even if He had an intelligent purpose in creating us, no one really knows what this purpose might be, or that it is especially meaningful.

The Second Law of Thermodynamics states that the entropy of a closed system—including the universe itself—increases up to the point at which equilibrium is reached, and God's purpose in creating us, and, indeed, all of nature, might have been no more lofty than to catalyse this process much as soil organisms catalyse the decomposition of organic matter.

If our God-given purpose is to act as super-efficient heat dissipators, then having no purpose at all is better than having this sort of purpose—because it frees us to be the authors of our purpose or purposes and so to lead truly dignified and meaningful lives.

In fact, following this logic, having no purpose at all is better than having any kind of pre-determined purpose, even more traditional, uplifting ones such as serving God or improving our karma.

In short, even if God exists, and even if He had an intelligent purpose in creating us (and why should He have had?), we do not know what this purpose might be, and, whatever it might be, we would rather be able to do without it, or at least to ignore or discount it. For unless we can be free to become the authors of our own purpose or purposes, our lives may have, at worst, no purpose at all, and, at best, only some unfathomable and potentially trivial purpose that is not of our own choosing.

You or others might object that not to have a pre-determined purpose is, really, not to have any purpose at all. But this is to believe that for something to have a purpose, it must have been created with that particular purpose in mind, and, moreover, must still be serving that same original purpose

Life in the concentration camp taught Frankl that our main drive or motivation in life is neither pleasure, as Freud had believed, nor power, as Adler had believed, but meaning. After his release, Frankl founded the school of logotherapy (from the Greek logos, meaning "reason" or "principle"), which is sometimes referred to as the "Third Viennese School of Psychotherapy" for coming after those of Freud and Adler. The aim of logotherapy is to carry out an existential analysis of the person, and, in so doing, to help her uncover or discover meaning for her life.

According to Frankl, meaning can be found through:

- Experiencing reality by interacting authentically with the environment and with others.

- Giving something back to the world through creativity and self-expression, and,

- Changing our attitude when faced with a situation or circumstance that we cannot change.

- "The point," said Frankl, "'is not what we expect from life, but rather what life expects from us."

We are constantly asked and/or asking what the meaning of life is. Truly, the answer will vary from person to person, it all depends on whom you are directing the question to. One might say that the meaning of life is money, for it is without it that we cannot survive. Another might say that it is friends or family, that very bond that we enjoy is the meaning of life. And another individual might say that it's love that is the meaning of life.In reality, no one really knows and there really isn't a direct answer to the question. To me, however, the meaning of life is about being who you are and being that well. Living each day truly well and being grateful for being on this side of the grass; never taking any day or anything nor anyone for granted. My Catholic School background taught me that and those quotes are taken from Saint Francis de Sales. Even if you are not a Catholic or a Christian for that matter, those quotes can still be put into practice by you regardless of your creed.

Being who you are and being that well is all about putting your talents to use and never taking them for granted. Realizing that you are unique and put here for a purpose. Everyone has talents and gifts, but not everyone uses them. I know at times I don't use my talents to their ability, but I'm trying. Some people's talents are those of great measure, some talents are little things that aren't always recognized, whatever the case may be, put them to good use. They might come in handy someday.

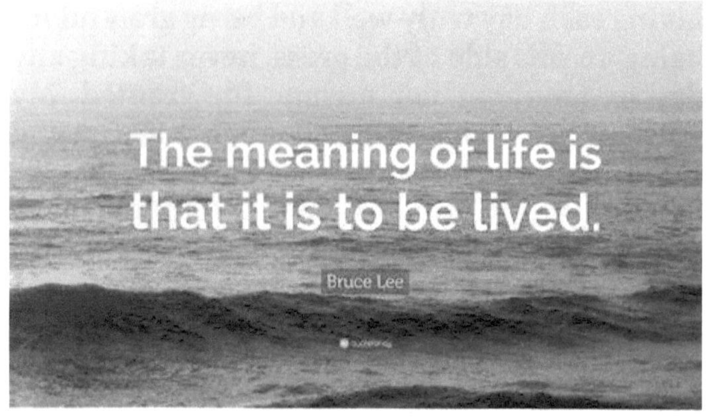

Living each day well can be a difficult task for the simple reason that life isn't always as predictable as we want it to be. Things happen, moods change, but the most important thing to realize is that we must appreciate the little things in life. The little things like where we are at this very moment while we're reading this article; the little things like who is important in your life. If someone is important or you love them, tell them. You might never get the chance to do it again. Tomorrow is promised to no man.

Finally, Carpe Diem. Seize the day. That is what life's all about. Seeing an opportunity and going after it knowing damn well that you have a chance to fail. Dare to fail and truly, nothing can go wrong.

"Sip your Tea Nice and Slow

No-one Ever knows when it's Time to Go,

There'll be no Time to enjoy the Glow,

So sip your Tea,Nice and Slow.

Life is too Short butfeels pretty Long,

There's too much to do, so much going Wrong,

And Most of the Time You Struggle to be Strong,

Before it's too Lateand it's time to Go,

Sip your Tea Nice and Slow.

Some Friends stay, others Go away,

Loved ones are Cherished but not all will Stay.

Kids will Grow upand Fly away.

There's really no Saying how Things will Go,

So sip your Tea ,Nice and Slow.

ᗐᗐᗐ

3
Be Happy

♡

Instead of jumping out of bed and rushing right into stress of what we need to do... breathe... take a moment to eliminate the stress and re-align your mind,body and brain with joy that does live inside you. you get to choose if your day if your day is going to be live every other day,or if it is going to be a great day. we have to decide first thing in morning, by giving yourself that time,to re-align your brain to positiviy,to re-direct mind to what is good in your life. start your day with INTENSION . TODAY i will be present.TODAY I will be kind. TODAY I will be the example.its all about intention if your focus is towards good you will be more... if you want to be really happy: give thing . happy peoples are grateful people.so spend time in gratitude. spend time in intension and expectation fell mind withh positivity, attract intensions, beliefs and attracr what you feel.so get up and feel good.

Today is a new day. A fresh , clean canvas. You can paint whatever you want on that canvas no matter what happens. You are the artist. ADD some color,some joy ,some life to your canvas leave nothing off that canvas! instead of worring all time go and ask to yourself that really it is more better than ever loving your life when you learn to love your life , life will love you ,come up with with some blossoms make your mind full of happiness take to world of joy make it elated. when you will be happy incidents in your life will happen according to you , face each and every problems and difficulties with happiness

your living becomes easier and you start being part of this beautifull world you contribute your happiness in this world and make others too ... always be passionate try to overcome worries and stress try to defeat them with your one smile . the best weapon for ever is your smile. happiness is the best makeup. its not that each and every pearson is happy in his or hers life we all have some kind of stresss which is always distrubing us from our happy life but the solution is not to be in stress and worries the way is in you . life is just like a game you get somewhere lose and some wins too.. so its not the case to be happy when you win , when you lose you get a chance to improve . Our life is short we all should know it. There is nothing you can not do, be or have. if there is someone even one person on this planet that has done it before, that means you can do it doesnt mean it is easy but it is not impossible. you can work to it and make your life abundant and happy. When the word IMPOSSIBLE is broken down it states that I M POSSIBLE. Nothing is worth it if it doesnt make you happy. whatever you are doing in that task if you are not happy doing that , if it doesnt makes you happy it not worth.just about everything worth fighting for is going to require a real fight to win a prize. you will have to suffer no doubt in that and you need to sacrifice for almost anything worthwhile in life but you should ask yourself this question about everything you do in your life does this make me happy? if the answer is no. ask yourself will this sacrifice I am making lead more happiness in long term if not you shoul let it go. be yourelf . BE YOURSELF the only way to be happy in your life is if you be you !you will be never happy in your life if you are constantly doing things to please others, to compete with others or to be liked another. actually you are UNIQUE and that is your greatest gift. when you follow your own path,regardless with others you open up space for great things to enter your life. compare your self with no one . make your own decisions and it will lead you to great life. Every thing you need is already within you . in this life we see many people who materially speaking but they are empty inside. Jerry Maguire says,"Needing nothing attracts everything". happiness is only and always found within us . Happiness is highest level of success SURROUND YOURSELF WITH GOOD PEOPLE. many peoples are arround you surrounding you some good and some are worst the worst people kill your positive energy but it is in your hand that letting them kill your positive energy but you have to live with your happiness. those who are truly aligned with you will never hold you back from living the life you want to live. dont dim your light shading with others shine bright. those who see your spark will shine with you. you cannot live a great life , a happy life, if you surround yourself with toxic peoples. If you search for negativity in this world , you will find plenty of it. if you search for hate , anger,violence and sadness you will find it But the same is true on the flip side; if your only intension is search for good you will find only th good whatever meaning you give yourlife becomes your life.It can be a failure or a lesson. heart break or character building. Most people drift through life with no sense of purpose,no direction or true joy.they pay no attention to fact they arent happy, and never address mindset and choices that led to their unhappiness, but if they did they might be able to reverse it. most people have LIMITING BELIEFS and so their life is LIMITED. they BELIEVE life is HARD they believe life is full of sadness and misery.They believe at some level, consiously or subconsiously their best days are behind them. they believe fitting it and wearing masks will get them a better or easier life, than being their true self and following their true passions. there happiness is depended on what happens they are not in control of life, life is in control of them. if you are able to switch your beliefs about life to these 7 empowerig beliefs, life was strt to work for you. the blessing will appear , the joy that is inside you will start rissing out.

1.

There are 7 beliefs to live a great life:"I decide how I feel, no matter the circumstances." have you ever notice people seem to get upset over just about anything? did you also notice that they seem to have a lot to be unhappy about? the truth is they let every little circumstances make them unhappy some cuts off in traffic... ruins their day. someone says something unkind... they replay it in their mind for weeks. when you adapt belief that you are in control over how you feel and you commit to do the daily work on yourself , two thing happens you become empowered and you know nothing has the power to make you unhappy.

2.

"I have so much to be thankful for" happy people are happy because they appreciate more than unhappy people. it has been said many times you can be happy with little or miserable with much. knowing this you understand the goal is never to accumulate wealth or things its to get it into place where you feel like you have everything. feel blessed and you will be blessed.

3.

"Being myself attracts right peoples" one of the greatest tragidies of human beings is that majority change who they are to fit into the world . they believe being like someone else, will make them fit in better with others, be liked by others... but the truth is, you'll never attract the right people by being someone you are not. be yourself, and the right people for you will show up. the right people will love the real you. Ralph Waldo Emerson once said;"to be yourself in a world that is constantly trying to make you something else is the greatest accomplishment." have the courage to be you. Always believe and know if you do so, the perfect people in circumstances will show up in your life!

4.

"I am capable of anything" Successful people, know with certainty anything they live can be their reality. Imagine what you could create in your life with the belief. "I AM CAPABLE OF ANYTHING". youare so believe it know it and apply it to find something you want. that dream you have plan for it. work for it and go get it.that change you have been putting off: believe you can do it and go for it!

5.

"Kindness always wins" "Kindness and Good always win when the clock hits 0:00" Being "kind", "good", and caring is how you leave a legacy. It's why kindness is one of my biggest values. I want the admiration. Sometimes people can get away with bad behavior in the short term, but kindness and positivity will always win the game.

6.

"Everyting is blessing or lesson" think of survival or disease or abuse that go though the worst kinds of pain ,but because of that pain they rise out of it of life they help to others how are suffering from same pain.you can learn from your past, you can use it. believe it was sent to make you stronger, better, more compassionate,believe that there was a reason for it.

7.

"My best is yet to come." What you achieve uptill now you got believe that your best is yet to come? Well guess what? YOUR BEST IS YET TO COME. look yourself in mirror nad tell to yourself that your best is yet to come. many times in your life there are best results you have ever achieved in that area but that doesnt mean you cant do even more better than it .

Sometimes we think that we would be happy if all our dreams come true. However, it's the process of achieving our goals and it's the road towards our dreams that enriches us and makes us happy.There was a little, but always cranky girl. Everything was bad for her. It wasn't enough toys, the gifts she was getting were wrong. She wished to meet an enchantress that would turn her life a fairy tale.One day an enchantress came to the little girl and said that she will fulfil one of her wishes. The girl became very happy at first, but then she started to think: she had a lot of wishes and all of them were important for her. The girl thought for a long time, she could not choose just one. Then kind enchantress said that she gives her the fulfilment of one wish every day. The girl became happier: now all her dreams will come true. She thanked kind enchantress and ran home.

From that day she was waiting for every morning with joy and enthusiasm: because one more dream will come true for her. The days passed, the dreams came true... But soon the little girl realized that fulfilment of the wishes does not give her joy and happiness which she hoped for. Many wishes brought her disappointment, and some even a pain. Almost every dream was an empty little girl's caprice. Being satisfied, she suddenly realized that she did not want this.

The girl was getting sadder and sadder day by day, and wish-fulfilment did not bring any joy to her. Soon she started to fear her own dreams.

So the girl went to the kind enchantress and asked her to take her terrible gift back. She was afraid to live, afraid to wake up every day, waiting for an imminent execution of another wish. Crying, she asked an enchantress to fulfil only one her dream: to live as she lived before and enjoy life. And that her many wishes would remain only the wishes, from which she will select the one she will bring to her life.

Kind enchantress had mercy upon the little girl. She waved her magic wand and disappeared. The girl ran home. She was happy, because she knew that now she would laboriously seek for her one big cherished dream, not wasting time with short-term, in fact, quite unnecessary whims.

4

Humanity for humans

HUMANITY FOR HUMANS

Actually I believed for sometimes that are humans made for their own sake of happiness our for others

. probably as per me humanity is nothing but a perspectives behaviour in which humans should behave and they must go on

In that way it is obviously a thing of great concern we neglect that thing in our daily schedule but it can lead to a big and humourous problem

Now what is the problem that i am talking about is we all live in a planet earth this planet is so big and it has diverse culture, castes, states ,country and everything we see is different from other but i don't love my planet i want a planet in which no one will be discriminated on any basis of anything . i imagine of a planet where no one is more than other .

I want a planet ,

Where none is more than one,

No one is crying or lying

Everyone is happy and content.

I want a planet ,

In which where everyone is blissfull,

No one is sad or lad

Everyone is laughing and enjoying.

I want a planet ,

Where there is no caste nor religion,

No one is discriminated

Everyone is equal for one another.

-PRANJAL BORKAR

The first meaning of humanity describes a particular kind of animal that biologists encouragingly call homo sapiens – or wise human – and which seems distinct from all other animals because of its powers of language, reasoning, imagination and technology. This biological and evolutionary use of the term has the same meaning as "humankind" and marks us out as a particular life form that is different to other kinds of animal and vegetative life.

The power of the human species is considerable over the non-human world. This is mainly because our intelligence has consistently invented and deployed tools and technology which means we have come to dominate the earth, and our imagination has shaped religious and political meanings around which we form competing interests and social movements.

Our tools mean we are not a simple species but always function as a hybrid species – part human and part technology – in a constantly changing mix of human and non-human components. This hybrid humanity must infuriate non-human life like lions and microbes who could easily "take us down" in a fair fight of simple life forms, but who have consistently encountered us in hybrid forms in which we merge our humanity with spears, guns, horses, cars, vaccines and antibiotics.We operate routinely in these human-machine interactions (HMI) of various kinds. I am doing it now typing on my Macbook Air with an electric fan to keep me cool on a hot summer's day. Our mechanization gives us exponential power and unfair advantage over non-human life forms both large and microscopic, which tend to remain simple in one form except for bacteria and viruses, our most threatening predators, which can change form relatively fast.Our essential hybridity with other animal, plant and machine life is now in the emergent stages of a giant leap towards new forms of power which we cannot envision. New applications of biotech, robotics and artificial intelligence (AI) mean that our hybrid humanity is about to expand exponentially in a way that is already changing what it means to be human. Today's technologists are focused hard on simplifying human-machine interfaces – different types of "dashboards" which use our five human senses and recognize human gestures so that our humanity interacts seamlessly with AI of various kinds. These interfaces will increasingly be embedded in our bodies and minds as new levels of interactivity with technology which will inevitably change the experience of being human and the power of humanity.

Technology will not just change us where we are but also change where we can be. Humanity will be enhanced in time and space but also relocated across time and space. For example, because I am on Twitter or Skype, I can already be visibly present elsewhere, speaking and responding in thousands of different places across time and space. This is radically different from my great grandmother who could only ever really be visible and engaged in one place at one time, or in two places at two times when someone far away was reading a letter from her.

This time-space compression and its resulting context collapse which began with radio and television is an ever-increasing feature of being human. Some of our grandchildren will probably be talking and listening simultaneously in a hundred different places at once in embodied replicas as holograms or humanoid drones. They will probably be fluent in all languages, move through space much faster than us and live forever on earth and in space because of biological and AI enhancements. Our machines will develop new levels of autonomy which, although created by humans, are inevitably adapted by machine learning into new forms of non-human and non-animal life.This all means that the power of humanity as a species is about to increase dramatically because of a revolution in human-machine interaction which will see new forms of hybridity beyond our current imagining. Our human power will become even greater but what about our wisdom and the way we use this new power of humanity? In short, what about the ethics of our behaviour in our new hybrid humanity?Over the last 200 years, a third sense of humanity has increasingly referred to a single global identity across all human societies. This is not a simple biological identity but the idea that as a conflicted species we can and must build a single global political identity in which every human has a stake. This global identity is a meta identity which transcends smaller identities shaped by culture, nation, class, political opinion and religion.

The purpose of this single political humanity is to build a human "we" in which can share a common species consciousness as one group sharing a single planetary "home" and so work together on common problems and common opportunities that face the whole of humanity.

This political sense of being a single global group is experiencing push-back today as a broad-based politics of ethnic and economic nationalism expresses scepticism about globalism of all kinds. This political turn sees many people asking national politicians to think "more about us here" and "less about them over there". But our Movement continues to argue that it is important to imagine and build a global sense of humanity because our common human problems are intense and interdependent, and can only be solved internationally not just nationally.There are five truly existential problems that we all share as members of the human species, and always have done. Threats from each one can be significantly reduced if we work together to solve them in the spirit of Dumas' Three Musketeers: "all for one and one for all". This is what we try to do at the International Conference. Our perennial five problems are:

1. The problem of our violence as a species as it plays out terribly in war and violent crime.
2. Our struggle for fairness and our desire to reduce inequalities between us.
3. Our predators and their threat to our health which now take mainly microscopic form as

infectious microbes, or chronic and autoimmune diseases in which we attack ourselves.

4. Our relationship with the non-human environment and its impact on human survival.

5. The promethean risk of our creativity and how our technological inventions help and harm as they change the world around us and redefine humanity itself in new hybrid forms.

These five deep species problems will all be raised in various forms at our Conference in December. They will require a powerful response by all humanity, with an ethic of humanity, to ensure the survival of humanity.

Humanity as ethical behaviour

We now come to the another meaning of humanity which is used to describe a certain moral value that we can see operating across humankind as kindness and compassion for one another. We can therefore understand this second meaning as the kindness of humans. This humanity is our first Fundamental Principle and primary purpose in the Red Cross and Red Crescent Movement and has been summarized as follows since 1965:

"To prevent and alleviate human suffering wherever it may be found (and) to protect life and health and ensure respect for the human being."

This principle of humanity is the fundamental value at play in every Red Cross and Red Crescent worker wherever they are in the world today. If you stop one of them in whatever they are doing – taking blood donations in a major city, organizing relief in war or disaster, or negotiating with diplomats in the UN Security Council – and ask them why they are doing it, each one them should simply answer: "I am trying to protect life and health and ensure respect for human beings."

This is humanity in action and it is the power of this humanity – humane behaviour towards other humans – that we seek to celebrate, improve and increase in our Movement's 33rd International Conference in December.

Humanity in this sense is human behaviour that cares for other humans because of a profound and universally held conviction that life is better than death, and that to live well means being treated humanely in relationships of mutual respect. This commitment is a driving principle in the rules of behaviour in the Geneva Conventions, whose 70th anniversary falls this year, and in the Disaster Laws recommended by the Movement to ensure better disaster prevention, preparedness and response around the world.

The Red Cross and Red Crescent Movement is at once symbol, advocate and embodiment of this ethic of humanity and so is constantly working emotionally, judicially and practically to increase humanity as a dominant form of human behaviour in extreme situations. This is not easy, of course, because the human species is ethically ambivalent and not simply driven by an ethic of humanity. We are also deeply competitive, cruel and violent as a species and often believe that some things we have constructed are much more important than particular human lives. The reason that the call for humanity is so loud is because our record of inhumanity is so long, and the power of inhumanity is often greater than the power of humanity.

And what of humanity's behaviour towards non-human life? In our era of climate crisis, environmental degradation and multiple species extinction, the moral principle of humanity is looking increasingly self-referential and incomplete as a primary ethic for the human species. Quite simply, it is not enough for humans only to be kind to humans.

The principle of humanity as currently expressed is a classic example of speciesism in ethics. It cares only about one species – our own. We may claim that the principle of humanity is a niche ethic for calamitous human situations which rightly trumps wider ethical considerations in extremis, but this is neither true nor realistic. It is not true because the principle of humanity already takes account of the natural environment in the laws of war and the norms of disaster response and so recognizes the importance of non-human life in its own right and as means to human life. Nor is it realistic at a time when our biggest existential challenge as a species arises from our relationship with the non-human world around us.

The principle of humanity must, therefore, keep pace with the ethical evolution of humanity (the species) and needs to expand its purpose and behaviour towards non-human life. This currently includes all animal and vegetative life. But, in future, it is increasingly also likely to include non-human machines like robots and AI which may develop their own levels of consciousness, feelings and rights as they increasingly merge with humanity – the species and its ethics – in hybrid forms.

Here time is pressing. We may have little time to work out what it means to apply humane behaviour within non-human machines and towards non-human machines. This means agreeing how non-human machines and new models of human-machine interactions can behave with humanity, especially as new weapons systems. It will also mean thinking about how we should show humanity to increasingly machine-like humans and human-like machines.

We may have even less time to think hard about what it means to show humanity to non-human environments and animals in the Movement's humanitarian norms and work. At the moment, our humanitarian action can be profoundly inhumane to non-human life, neither protecting nor respecting it.

With all this uncertainty about what exactly it may mean to be human in future and the persistent record of our inhumanity to each other and towards non-human life, what sense does it make to try to aspire to a single global identity as billions of human beings?

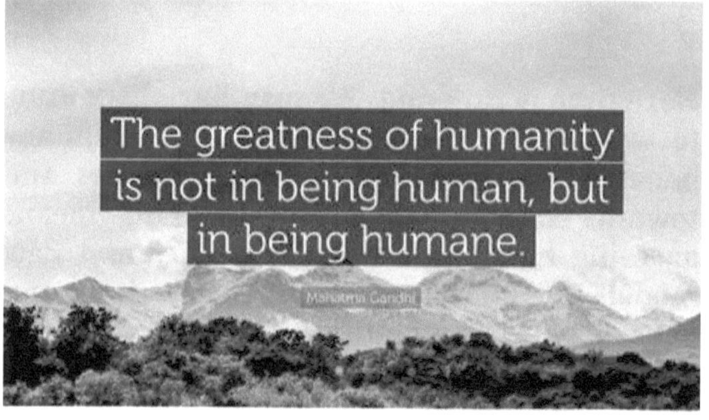

5

what matters?

We live in a world packed with material possessions and are encouraged to chase these things. As a result, our needs never seem to stop growing. So we keep running. But what really matters here?

We run after bigger television sets, newer smartphones, and better cars. We run after job promotions and luxurious holidays. We tend to think that more money in our bank accounts will translate into happier lives. While offline and online shopping can bring us short-term satisfaction, it rarely matters in the long run. There are all examples of things that don't matter in the end.

Well then, what really matters in life?

What really matters in life

The wise do not chase after materialistic items. More clothes, smarter gadgets, bigger cars, and luxurious houses can make our lives more convenient, but do these things bring us long-lasting happiness?

They don't.

What really matters in life is happiness itself. Happiness comes from having a purpose in life, loving and accepting yourself and others, and maintaining good health. Without these, you will always end up feeling unfulfilled and unhappy.

Research on the impact of relationships on life

An adult development study by Harvard on the lives of more than 700 people was conducted for over 75 years. The participants were divided into two groups - one group with participants who finished college and the other with participants from poor neighborhoods. Their personal and professional lives were studied, as well as their health and relationships.

While most people thought that money and fame made for a happier life, the research showed something different. It was good relationships that had a more positive impact on life. It's not about having a big circle of friends or several relationships. It's about having meaningful relationships. Quality over quantity.

In the words of Professor Robert Waldinger, the director of the study:

The clearest message that we get from this 75-year study is this: Good relationships keep us happier and healthierThe researchers tracked data from 2006 and 2010 from a national study of participants over 50 years old. Physical and psychological examinations of their health were conducted, including walking speed, grip test, and a questionnaire to measure their sense of purpose. The results showed that the participants with a higher sense of purpose had a reduced risk of developing weaker grip and slower speed.

Purpose in life

A sense of purpose gives us the "why" of our life. It is the reason why we do what we do. It is the reason for our actions, our work and our relationships. Our lives revolve around this purpose. It gives our life meaning - a meaning which matters in life.

However, do not panic if you struggle to find your purpose. We have all been in that place. I remember when I did, I asked myself three questions:

Why do I get up?

What do I want?

What do I not want?

These questions have helped me find my purpose in life. It helped me discover what really matters to me. Whenever you feel like you are losing track of your life and yourself, you can always go back to these questions. Just remember to be honest with yourself.

2. Good relationships

Relationships are important. The positive kind, of course. In a busy world like ours, we often think that we don't have a lot of time to give to our family or friends.

Even worse, we take it all for granted and postpone it for later, while we prioritize our work.

However, your family, friends, and loved ones are part of what makes your life happier.

Good relationships are a crucial part of a happy life.

I remember the happiest memories of my life revolve around spending time with my family and friends.

Good relationships really matter. You need to nurture these relationships with the attention, love, and care that they deserve.

Here are a few ways to do that:

Spend time with people who support and encourage you.

Replace the time you spend on your phone or TV with real people.

Do things with your loved ones to strengthen your relationship with them.

Reach out to old friends and relatives and connect with your colleagues.

Spend time with positive people and watch how it changes your life for the better.

3. Good health

Health is probably one of the most important things that we take for granted. We don't eat healthily, we sleep poorly, and we don't treasure our bodies. But health matters - both our physical health and mental health.

Be kind to yourself, your mind, and your body. A lot of people are not so lucky to have a healthy body, so keep it nourished and nurtured.

Here are some interesting articles filled with tips on how to focus on your health:

How Much Does Exercising Make You Happier? (Research + Tips)

Mental Benefits Of Walking: Here's Why It Makes You Happier!

4 Ways To Find Happiness Through Yoga (From A Yoga Teacher)

Always prioritize your health. Improve your lifestyle. Eat healthily and drink plenty of water. Get out and talk to people. Visit the doctor for regular check-ups. Treat your health as if it is crucial because it really is.

4. Love and accept yourself

Accepting and loving yourself matters. When you completely embrace yourself and nurture your well-being and growth, you'll start to see the positive effect it has on your life. A positive view of yourself leads to a positive view of the world.

Don't be afraid to be yourself and accept yourself for who you are.

If you are unable to love yourself, you will be unable to love others too. There was a time in my life when I criticized everything I did and thought that my life fell apart because of how I am. I disliked myself. Not long after, I started distancing myself from people. It was after I learned how to love myself that I could love and care for others.

How did I do that?

I accepted my flaws and recognized my strengths.

I forgave myself when I made a mistake, but I also held myself accountable.

I spent time with those I loved and asked for help when I needed it.

I stayed positive as much as I could and let go of resentment.

I made healthier choices and tracked my growth and progress.

In short, I started to love myself again, and so can you. Take time to discover your true self and embrace it.

6

Experience teach us

Here I would like to tell my own experience with that I understood about the living life of humans aswell as I am studying in grade 8 at podar international school washim . I got my inspiration my history teacher pravin sir he teaches me Social Science but once while teaching he told one thing from that day I strated to live not only for me but for others too he was teaching us about our indian constitution that how are indian constitution is formed and whatever changes can take place in consttitution and whatever changes have been taken in constitution so that time he told us that how the people of ancient time were and the situation before constitution was formed and we were not having our freedom and our independence actually that ay I got that before independence the people were surving but without there freedom and they were no more any ruler of there mind and their brain but today we are ... but we dont take advantage of todays situation . so that day a question arised in my mind they were living that time and some of the great freedom fighters sacrificed there life too ... and today also they are between us we say . as we I mean todays generation we are living still we dont do anything which will make us alive stillwe die . all I mean to say is our living or surving must have a purpose as we survive but what is reason behind that that is main and very important thing . I also know that our life is just temporary but yes he cannot live here as permanant one but yes we can make our place in others mind that even we are not there they will have us in them . being the reason for our own happiness is different and being the reason for others happiness is different . so be the reason for others happuness be the reason for pthers smile be the reason fr others smile.when we make others happy ultimately happiness comes to "as you ,you reap " it clearly means that as you perform the activities in your schedule the result will be ultimate if we think good about others , others will do better of us.being bad person is worst thing but being a good one is best thing so always we need to decide that we need to do . here I would give one example once our exams were there and my hisorty teacher I mean pravin sir he saw that some students were cheating in exam so one thing he told which always makes me honest and reminds me that you are not going to be less than your marks he told that day " students your marks will not decide your knowldge." yes to this I would say that yes the marks we get in exams they will not decide our knowldge but yes if it is about the exam deciding our future we need to score good but it doesnt mean we have to do cheating because it is better to fail than to do cheating because failures are pillars to success as you fail you understand the mistake and next time you try to overcome with that . here I remember once my father told me that this world what you see with your eyes is just a picture infront of you if you dont exist in that world if you dont do any sort of positive thing if you dont be a good person . before achiving any aim or ambition in our life our first ambition must be to be a human , to be a person . the person is one of living thing on earth who is honest, polite, kind, etc... but I to feel that I also miss this we say that no one can be perfect and we also say that practice makes man perfect so being perfect here it means is giving our 100% will atleast give us 99% so in each thing we do we must give our level up to mark i that field talking about humanity so humanity is something which defines a human about his or her quality that humans possess actually.

Nothing teaches *us better than our own* experiences!

Also pravin sir told us that human life is only a life in which humans understand each others feelings and emotion and they are one of the creater of this humanity ,so humanity is for human even if tommorow humans die we have to keep our humanity alive as we die we are burried on ground of earth and then our energy we have that is also burried but that is not destroyed so that energy is conserved in same way we live we die but humanity within us must not die in same way it must be alive . we are the must lucky people to get life of humans

As humans are progressing as a human race into the future, the true essence of humanity is being corrupted slowly. It is essential to remember that the acts of humanity must not have any kind of personal gain behind them like fame, money or power.

The world we live in today is divided by borders but the reach we can have is limitless. We are lucky enough to have the freedom to travel anywhere and experience anything we wish for. A lot of nations fight constantly to acquire land which results in the loss of many innocent lives.

Similarly, other humanitarian crisis like the ones in Yemen, Syria, Myanmar and more costs the lives of more than millions of people. The situation is not resolving anytime soon, thus we need humanity for this.

Most importantly, humanity does not just limit to humans but also caring for the environment and every living being. We must all come together to show true humanity and help out other humans, animals and our environment to heal and prosper.

The Great Humanitarians

There are many great humanitarians who live among us and also in history. To name a few, we had Mother Teresa, Mahatma Gandhi, Nelson Mandela, Princess Diana and more. These are just a few of the names which almost everyone knows.

Mother Teresa was a woman who devoted her entire life to serving the poor and needy from a nation. Rabindranath Tagore was an Indian poet who truly believed in humanity and considered it his true religion.

Similarly, Nelson Mandela was a great humanitarian who worked all his life for those in needs. He never discriminated against any person on the basis of colour, sex, creed or anything.

Further, Mahatma Gandhi serves as a great example of devoting his life to free his country and serve his fellow countrymen. He died serving the country and working for the betterment of his nation. Thus, we must all take inspiration from such great people.

The acts and ways of these great humanitarians serve as a great example for us now to do better in our life. We must all indulge in acts of giving back and coming to help those in need. All in all, humanity arises from selfless acts of compassion.

As technology and capitalism are evolving at a faster rate in this era, we must all spread humanity wherever possible. When we start practising humanity, we can tackle many big problems like global warming, pollution, extinction of animals and more.

Life teaches u

Here i would like to tell a story . there was girl how has failed in here exams , she was very upset and hurted , her father noticed that and then he called her in kitchen . then the girl went with her father in kitchen . her father put three bowls on stove of same size and he put equal amount of water in that bowls , then he took few potatoes, eggs and coffee beans and then he put potatoes in one bowl, eggs in other bowl and coffee beans in third bowl , then he on the stove that time after 15 mins he off the stove and then he took out potatoes, eggs and then with tea strainer he strain the coffee beans with water . Girl was not understanding anything. Then her father told to touch each item with hand then potatoes were soft , egg will more strong as compare to before boiling it and coffee beans were strain . so from this we understand that whenever the problems come to us we have to decide that we have to decide that like whom we should be like potatoes that before problem in life we are strong and after the problem we start to feel weak from inside, like egg that after problem we start being more strong or like coffee beans we will start to feel strong as well we will change our life.

You can change yourself and your life

When I was in grade4 I remember I use to read sometimes newspaper that time I read there I use to come to the syntax there everyday about government , today government made this changes that changes , everyone need to follow that ,I use to come to it and once I asked my father that who is this government I also want to be a government and I also want to rule country I thought it something that government is a person and makes some changes in our life and our world .

I once went to a library and there were many books once shelf was with life books , in that there was one book in which it was written that read this book it will change your like I thought that really lets try it then I took that book and I started to read it , once upon a time the god was living with humans , that time humans complained to god some farmers said that when we want rain it doesn't comes and then the person who wants to wash his clothes he says that when I want to wash my clothes there it rains . Once a farmer was highly unsatisfied with god rules and management he said god you are not doing good management that time good gives him all powers to make all the management whatever he wants then the farmer to his crops he gave fertile land proper sunlight, rain and eventually proper environment for growth of plant then he saw his good crops he went to god and he said that god see how I grown the crops that time god said check once by taking out chaff from it there were no wheat and some wheat haven't grown properly , so that time farmer asked god that was there any trick behind this , so the god said no . then farmer asked why did this happen then so then god relied that there was no struggle of seed in whole process and the take home of story was we must know our potential ,our weakness and with failures we must rise on too, because life is full of struggle and once you start to struggle the life ultimately gives fruits of your struggle.

Life teaches us lessons, and such lessons are the keys to success. How far do you agree with this statement, and do you think formal education is essential or people should rely on their life experiences.People will learn several life lessons in their path towards success. They will learn it from their daily lifestyle. Also from their friends, family members, colleagues, partners, neighbours, role models. People learn these lessons from their mistakes, observation of any activity or someone. Nobody can teach someone these lessons, but someone can learn these lessons from successful people's activities and mistakes also their way of thinking. Once people start understanding life lessons, they can feel positivity in their life. Additionally, it will change their way of thinking. Once they start applying their life lessons, they will feel less stressed, more focused and more material. They can get success by little more hard work and believing in life lessons.

at every stage of life we learn from life, which is key for success. I completely agree with the given statement, if we learn from the past then a rare chance to repeat mistakes, beneficial for later in life. One debate about education vs life experiences, I think both are useful, education is beneficial in professional life while life experiences are in social life.situation and lesson set pathway of success, older people have the vast majority of experience and life lessons so they can handle any critical situation thus, companies hire them and yield healthy salary, as well as community, also prefer older people advice over youth.

7

Birth to Death

All living organisms born and they die . the way between birth and death is our life that we live actually . if you have marked in birth certificate the date of birth is written on left side while on death certificate the date of deat is written on right side so the way between this two date we have to surpass that. humans have did the discoveries of many things from bulb to electricity , from hydroelectricity to solar electricity, from refrigeratoe to invetor but one thing is still not discovered I think you got it that is nothing but the time which is passed . humans have discovered many things so they have discovered it because they knw that the time which they have passed is not going to come again so each and every second they spend they think on that and finally they have successed in their life and they made all discoveries for our better of today so isnt it now our duty to start doing some useful things not for our generation but for us . so it starts with today no tommorow no yestreday but today .

looking towards the example of benjamin franklin he is the one who discovered "static electricity" he use to sell books and he was having a stationary shop of books once a man came to his shop and he ask the cost of book to his reply the worker of benjamin was there he said it cost is 100 dollar, then the customer said can the amount be lessed or can you decrease a little . the worker said,"no sorry " then the customer started fighting for it he said call our owner so the worker called benjamin and then when benjamin came and when the customer asked him the price he said it costs 150 dollar to customers surprise he said your worker said it is for 100 dollar , then to benjamins reply he told him that yes he was it is for 100 dollar but you wasted my time and for my time you need to give 150 and if you now start arguging then you need to give 200 dollar then customer understood his mistake and he gave 150 dollar and he took leave from there. the discoverers knew it that there time is going to finish and they knew it at any moment they can die so every moment they live like end minute of their life and each and every moment they utilise. time will never stop and you need to go on like time. we must think each and every moment like end moment as at really last moment we think all mistakes we commeted in our whole we always think about our past because after death our whole life will be like history like past . now stop crying because life will also cry when you will die so it is better to be happy in life to make us more happy at every moment we live . make your life happy and try to make others happy . you know that one day you are going to die one day , yes you know that . death is not happier ting and people feel it as bad when we talk about death people say talk about talk about something else ,but death is reality , but there are thousand of people who die and yes one day everything will be over .

so live a happy life

what is one thing that both rich and poor people can buy? yes thats happiness . happiness depends upon you your happiness i in your hand that you need to be happy or sad. everything happens for a reson in our life , each and everything . our life is just like a movie you will not understand that what you are doing now is for what let the climax come to your life you will understand that why this happened with you and what was the purpose behind it. keep trust on god , it doesnt matters you keep faith in you or not but start having faith on god and good deads.

stop comparing yourself with others stop having jelousness about other stop comparing if someone is more rich than you then the thing is you start being jealous about that person but if he is rich than it doesnt mean that he is more happier a car cant bring happiness in your life yes it can but for 1 or 2 months not for your whole life. love yourself , start loving yourself if you see others doing that you will do that but no what you are start rising in your field what you are in start progressing in that because what others do that doesnt mean to you behave like you are the one who can do it and you must also try for . because onece you start loving yourself and being best for you not for others you will be the happiest person in world so be change that you.

her is one story which I woul like to tell there was a boy who was hungry for success all that he waant was success everthing which meaned to him was success. once his running competition was there and he was preparing for that the next day two boys with him came for running with hi they ranned with him and they boy winned . all people around him cheered for him but their was a old man who didnt showed any sentiments then next two boys came and they ran with him he won again and again the crowd waved at the boy now still the old man didnt show any sentiments then th e boy said is there any one who can race with me the old man came forward and then with him he brought one old lady and a blind man they both were unable to walk and the boy said is it a race and then old man said you start running and then boy ran and he winned both the lady and man were at starting line but this time crowd didnt show any type of sentiment and then the boy was in thinking that now one is ready to be part of my success , then again the old man said to run with them now this time he walked so slowly with them and they crossed finishing line toogether this time the crowd was cheerig for them , the old man told him that in your life if you will win always, then who was challenger for you in your life and with whom were you fighting .

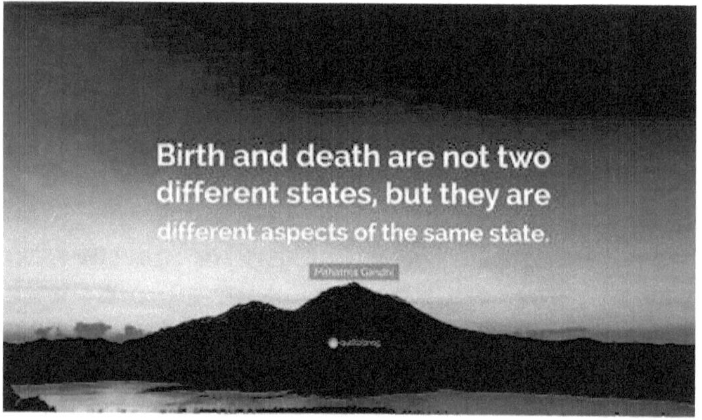

Enter Caption

8

Some are good , some are bad

One thing I have noticed that many people have that if you want something out of life if you want to change yourself , if you want to acquire something, if you something goal that you want to reach that is really not easy that some people make us feel that living your goal changing your behaviour , overcoming negative habits it is really challenging , it is hard, that living alone is very difficult it once we begin to come to grips with the fact that living is difficult, life is very challenging. I heard a song once by a guy named Gipples call if it ain't one thing it's another I say to you if it ain't one thing is 12 other always you will have problem in your life there will be no moment in life . one thing is that start being hungry start living for yourself you will find your way definetly you will . it is very important that you owe yourself I was reading a book by

Augmentee know called the university of success read one line gave me a chill I didn't have to read I don't have to read anything else in book he said." Of us never realize our greatness because we become sidetracked by secondary activity we spread ourselves top thin we don't know how to say no and we find ourselves doing all kind of things and never ever have time to do those things that we need to do to work on ourselves and then there goes second that goes another second, and we cant stop that each second and before you know it you wake up one day then you have your dreams bunch and your bills so decide that you are going to take some time to work on you that you deserve that from yourself that your life deserves some prime time because you are creating in your own production as Michael Todd would say you are starof your show you are the one riding the spirit and you will determine wheather your life is a good , better or best. Yes we all are humans and no one is there who never faced any problem in his or her life all are with full of problems and struggles which we need to fight with and we need to fight with but being one to fight with it and struggling with that problem is real superhero of his or her life . I know everyone are with problems no one can be happy forever in life but crying is not solution of that problem but trying is best answer of it as per me . Being a winner is something else but being fighter is first step of it and trying is very first step even when we born the first thing we do is we try to see this beautifull and astonishing world with our small eyes , thats what it teaches us to do all that we can , no one can be successful before trying and always this will not be that we will win some times we will lose while some time we will win but always winning will be not there because as we will win always it means you are not fighting with anyone in yourlife and you are just fighting with yourself I know that practice can bring perfection , but being perfect will start when you will start practicing and you will start doing things , you will not get solution of anything by sitting on place , not even you not even me and no one will get solution to problems on sitting on place.

As the first few lines of Benjamin Zephaniah's poem 'People Need People' tells us:

People need people,

To walk to

To talk to

To cry and rely on,

People will always need people.

Human beings are social beings; we need to interact with others; to connect and to feel that we belong and are valued. Having relationships with others is important; we need positive relationships. Who are the positive people in your life? Who do you enjoy spending time with? Who, for example, makes you laugh; is fun and lively to be with? Is there someone with whom you have shared interests? Who in your life is supportive and encouraging?

The positive people in your life do not just have to be friends or family; they could be colleagues or neighbours.The person you can talk to if you're worried could be your GP, a counsellor, someone at a support group or at the end of a helpline. Maybe the person who introduces you to new worlds, ideas, and interests is a tutor on a course or an author of interesting books.

Maybe it's someone on TV – David Attenborough and his programmes about wildlife or Brian Cox and his programmes about space, for instance. Perhaps there's a comedian on radio or TV who makes you laugh.Choosing to surround yourself with people who uplift you is a form of self-care.As Karl Marx advises; 'Surround yourself with people who make you happy. People who make you laugh, who help you when you're in need. People who genuinely care. They are the ones worth keeping in your life. Everyone else is just passing through.'

Connect with friends and family. Show interest, care, and concern. Keeping regular contact in person is good but even a message or phone call can make a difference.

Of course, having good relationships with others isn't something that just happens. You have to make time and effort.If you don't have good friends and family around you – if you need more positive relationships in your life – start to meet new people. One of the best ways to do this is to connect with people on shared interests. Of course, making new friends isn't always easy. But just as keeping friends takes time and effort, so does making new friends; you need to be willing to meet others, to be yourself and give something of yourself.Another way to connect with other people and experience positive relationships is through volunteering for a cause or local community initiative that interests you.

Doing something to benefit someone else can make you and the person you are helping feel good. Studies show that helping others creates feelings and attitudes that can lead to better physical health, better mental health, and overall happiness.

Volunteering is also a good way to meet people – other volunteers – and make friends. You can meet and create bonds with people who want to make a contribution to the lives of others; you have a common cause that is another opportunity to create meaning and purpose in your life.Volunteers can do almost anything: there's a huge range of volunteer opportunities available to you. Whether it's serving tea at a local hospice, helping at a local community food project or an animal rescue centre, working with refugees, advocating for someone with a learning disability or mental health problem, or mentoring people leaving the criminal justice system, not only can you make a contribution to other people's lives, but you can be involved in something that's relevant to your values and interests. It could be something related to politics, the environment and conservation, arts and music, or perhaps some voluntary work with older people, families, and children. See the 'Do It' website www.do-it.org for volunteering opportunities in the UK.

Let's be honest, we aren't able to handle the struggles of life by our lonesome. It would seem that people are strongest when they work together. Although sometimes there is nothing we can do about a specific group of people continually bringing us down.

That's why it's so important to surround ourselves with the right people. Ultimately, if we want to accomplish, achieve, grow, and be better, we need the people in our lives that will be along side to help us with the task!

Life is too short to choose complacency in friendships. We need to be encouraged, challenged, loved, and heard. If we want to continue to grow, the type of people that we choose to spend our time with becomes vital. We become who we spend our time with. There are a few types of people that we should be welcoming, and some that we should steer clear of.

Stay away from the gossipers

These "friends" will undoubtedly pull you down into their gossiping holes. If you have a lot of gossipers in your life, there's a good chance you lack a lot of genuine friends. These people are very good at appearing to be your best friend and creating what feels like an alliance with you.

Chances are, they are talking about you to someone else in the same regard. Be careful who you're around when you start talking about people. Avoid the chronic gossip as much as possible. It manifests into negativity and you can develop a very critical view of others. Gossiping leads to many negative roads that often don't allow U-turns. It creates a terrible habit that eventually leaves you as the one standing alone.

Stay away from chronic jealous people

It's difficult to have a bunch of friends that are constantly jealous of you. They often are not happy about your achievements, they will discourage and destroy your dreams, and they will try like hell to keep you at whatever underachieving level they occupy. The worst part — most of them don't even realize they're doing it.

It's not that they are always purposely discouraging you. They just can't help it sometimes. They don't want to see you succeed because they feel like theyshould be succeeding too. They want to tell you that your dream is dumb because they don't have one. It wouldn't be fair if you were able to work hard and achieve yours while they had to watch. It's more comfortable for them when you're in the same place because they're reassured that they aren't doing too badly. These people will often hold you back from pursuing the things in which you excel.

Stay close to motivated dreamers

Dreamers will most likely have your mindset. Do you want to create something? Do you want to pursue that dream job? Surrounding yourself with them will make the journey more bearable. They will consistently encourage you, because they know what adversity feels like.

They will be there at the end of your journey with a smile on their face. They are actually happy for you. When you fail, they will encourage you to get back up and take a different approach. They won't tell you to give up — they want you to succeed!

Stay close to optimism

Like dreamers, positive people want to see you succeed as well. They will be there to help in any way they can. Where they differ from dreamers — they often aren't chasing their own dream. Positive people are generally satisfied and content.

Having more optimism in your life is never a bad thing. Seeing the good in each situation, although easier said than done, will lead to a healthier mindset. Surrounding yourself with positive influences is a great start to making your daily life better.

9

Hurdles we need to come across

There are many people who will not see tomorrows life and tomorrow , time is something that no one can own . always remember that there is time meter which will start at every night and at second night it will again become zero zero so you need to do whatever you do in that one days time. All people know that time is very important . all people say that save time is it money that should be saved time is not saved it is used in primitive way . I have seen many people complaining that they don't have money but there are many successful people they know that more than money time is there and when you will understand that time is very important thing in your life that will be the very second you will even not like to waste that one second of your life . so think that what is time if you think it like theory of relativity then time will be very slow if you are fear that your is going fast then it will start running if there is any person who is even not having time to think about the time he is spending so this time will take him to very good position in his or her life after death of that person this will keep him alive on earth. Don't sit as it is do anything if for you dance matters than dance , if for you your hobbies are important then give time to your hobbies start giving time to them , because time travelling if in your life your goal earlier nothing will happen but if you will achieve it late you will be not able to enjoy that . you know that one thing that no one was got that is tomorrow , what is the thing that al think when they don't get something , they think that I must have done this in past . whatever must be your age but if you know importance of time then you are one the most punctual person of the world because when there is time with you you don't have the understanding power but when you have that understanding power that time you don't have time. Always remember that how much time you waste , time will waste you that much do anything but don't pass the time . so respect time , so time will give you whatever you want . every person who waste time is going to be waste who have wasted time in history he himself was wasted . the principle of time is same and equal for everyone this is same for bill gates and beggar, this is same for prime minister and for each citizen no one can stop time . if you don't gave time to your dreams then dreams will remain dreams forever never they will be reality. People say that time is not visible but makes many things visible infront of us. One day we need to die and once we die we will not get back to world when you will die it will not make anymore changes in world it will rotate as it was people will not stop living for you for some days they will miss you but again they will start to live that time you will understand that what was the real meaning of life and what is the meaning of life so you will understand that time hat I cant afford a new car, I cant give time to my family, you will understand that how much important was one second, one minute and one hour of your life . when time will give you then you will understand that what was meaning of time now everything that matters is time we all make dramatic act that I have this and that work I was not having time so what you do in 24 hrs have you asked this question to yourself anytime , ever have you asked the question to yourself that what you did in last whole week , in last whole month no because in that things we don't want to waste our time all want is doing time pass. The worst world in this planet is time pass . everything we start procrastinating it we say that tomorrow we will do this , everything we through on tomorrow and everything we need is we want to enjoy yes I know enjoying life is very important but if you will work today then you can enjoy your tomorrow so work hard now stop doing time pass . success comes to you when you work hard when ,work for it more than hoping for . as you will give more than need you will ultimately get results for it everything you do will give you results . expect little give much as you expect for the thing then you will just expect for it and you will be just expecting the result which you are eager for will be just a expectation. If you want that expectation to become a reality then start working for it get up and work for it. So get up and work for it , and always remember that wasting time will not bring any certain results so start doing it .

This is life; you face problems every day no matter how perfect you think you and your life are. Problems are there and they aren't going anywhere unless you face them and solve them. Acknowledging your problems, solving them, and getting on with your life is better than making it all a big deal. Your problems shouldn't become the source of sorrow, hurt, and grief for you.

While getting on with our life, we may encounter plenty of barriers and issues that might distract us from our real path. Sometimes we don't have our full potential to deal with the issues but if we know what we are dealing with, we can do better. Once you have a clear perspective of what problems you have in your life, you can deal with them in a better way.

10
life defines

journey we are all on is a varied one, for sure, but there are some similar things we are all going through.

Each of us, in our search for meaning in life, has a vast amount of experience to draw upon. Our struggles and hardships, along with our achievements and blessings, teach us life's lessons. Your experience, your strength and the hope that

Life is the aspect of existence that processes, acts, reacts, evaluates, and evolves through growth (reproduction and metabolism). The crucial difference between life and non-life (or non-living things) is that life uses energy for physical and conscious development. Life is anything that grows and eventually dies, i.e., ceases to proliferate and be cognizant. Can we say that viruses, for example, are cognizant? Yes, insofar as they react to stimuli; but they are alive essentially because they reproduce and grow. Computers are non-living because even though they can cognize, they do not develop biologically (grow), and cannot produce offspring. It is not cognition that determines life, then: it is rather proliferation and maturation towards a state of death; and death occurs only to living substances.

Or is the question, 'What is the meaning (purpose) of life?' That's a real tough one. But I think that the meaning of life is the ideals we impose upon it, what we demand of it. I've come to reaffirm my Boy Scout motto, give or take a few words, that the meaning of life is to: Do good, Be Good, but also to Receive Good. The foggy term in this advice, of course, is 'good'; but I leave that to the intuitive powers that we all share.

There are, of course, many intuitively clear examples of Doing Good: by retrieving a crying baby from a dumpster; by trying to rescue someone who's drowning. Most of us would avoid murdering; and most of us would refrain from other acts we find intuitively wrong. So our natural intuitions determine the meaning of life for us; and it seems for other species as well, for those intuitions resonate through much of life and give it its purpose.

Of all Webster's definitions of 'life', the one for me that best covers it is, "the sequence of physical and mental experiences that make up the existence of an individual." Indeed, life is a continuum of accomplishment, failure, discovery, dilemma, challenge, boredom, sadness, disappointment, appreciation, the giving and receipt of grace, empathy, peace, and our reactions to all sorts of stimuli – touch, love, friendship, loss... One can either merely exist or try to achieve, working through the difficult times, perhaps learning a thing or two. Everyone has a story. I've been surprised when learning something new about an acquaintance or friend that must have been very difficult to manage or survive; but there they are in front of me. It's how you come out on the other side of those challenging times that is important. How you land, get on with it, and keep on truckin'.

Life cannot be planned: there's fate, and there's simple bad luck. Failure can bring crushing disappointment, or you can try and make a new plan. A person can waste an inordinate amount of time mourning what they don't have, or plans that don't work out. But who wants to waste that much time regretting?

Life has happy surprises, small moments to cherish. It's a matter of weighing the good and bad times – the challenge is to balance both, ending up with a life looked back on that was worth the mighty effort. I'm not meaning to sound like a Pollyanna – I assure you I'm not – it's just more pleasant to strive for a modicum of equilibrium. If I can manage that, I'm good.

"Life's but a walking shadow, a poor player,
That struts and frets his hour upon the stage
And then is heard no more. It is a tale
Told by an idiot, full of sound and fury,
Signifying nothing."
(Macbeth, Act V, Scene V)

These words of Shakespeare's Macbeth summarize interesting ideas about the nature of life. The first line expresses two of the three marks of existence as per Buddhist thinking, Anicca, impermanence, and Anatta, non-self: a "walking shadow" is as insubstantial and impermanent as anything imaginable; a "poor player" neither creates nor directs his role, and the character being played only exists because of an author. Macbeth's entire statement, particularly the last sentence, expresses the third Buddhist mark of existence: Dukkha, dissatisfaction.

The stage metaphor in the second line represents boundaries or limits. Scientific research into the nature of life often focuses on the material, energetic, and temporal limitations within which life can exist. The temporal limit of life is known as death. In the spirit of this interpretation, the idea of being "heard no more" could imply that life constantly evolves new forms while discarding older ones.

Macbeth hints at the wisdom of mystery traditions while anticipating the revelations of genetic science by stating that life "is a tale". Now, this refers to the language-based, or code-based, nature of life. Readers may consider this in relation to DNA and RNA, and also in relation to John's Gospel: "In the beginning was the Word, and the Word was with God, and the Word was God." (The implications of the phrase "told by an idiot" exceed the scope of this inquiry.)

11

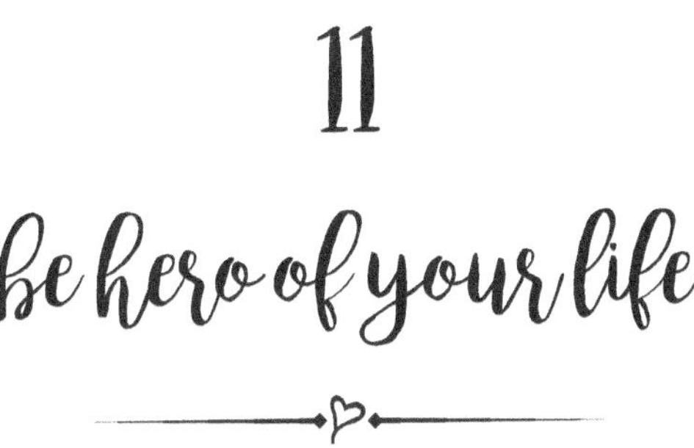

It is time to be hero in your own story.

I recently listened to an amazing interview Ed Mylett had with Robin Sharma. Robin is a mega author who wrote, "The Monk Who Sold His Ferrari." He wrote this book in story form and it was easy to understand...I actually read it to my three daughters as well.

Most recently, Robin wrote a book titled "The Everyday Hero Manifesto" in which he talks about mindset shifts needed in order to become your own hero...it REALLY resonated with me, so I figured I'd create content around this topic to raise your awareness of this fascinating concept.

But first...some super quick background info. Robin is a very successful author who has dedicated the last 20 years to seeing how much he can improve himself. He's had a lot of coaches over the years and has done extensive research in order to write this book. Before he got into the personal development space, he was an attorney that got burned out on the job.

His lessons really resonate with me because they are so concrete...and he is a master storyteller. You can also tell he eats his own dog food and has put a lot of time and money into improving himself.

Why It's Important To Be Your Own Hero

Being the hero of your own life means you take full responsibility for making yourself the best version you can be for yourself and for those around you. It's a worthwhile goal and the mission is to try and improve 1% every day.

When you become your own hero, you'll become the person your family, friends, and the world need. Why wouldn't you want to become better than what you are today? Especially if it means having a lasting impact on others?

Maybe you are letting your fears of uncertainty hold you back. It might scare you to think about the changes you need to make to become your own hero.

Take Small Actions Even When You Don't Feel Ready

I want to encourage you to embark on this mission even if you're not fully ready. I've had to do this myself and remind myself that if I wait until I feel like doing something...I'll likely never feel ready. Don't wait until XYZ is in place...instead–just start moving forward.

Doing the right thing when you don't feel like it can change the way you feel. Sometimes you have to take action in order for you to be excited about doing it. It's like working out...once you start working out, you typically feel more motivated to keep going.

Daily routines are really important for you to see progress on your goals. So on that note, here are the strategies you can put in place to become your own hero:

1. Take Full Responsibility

Whether good or bad, your life is the sum of the habits you have in place. Change is hard and it won't be easy to kill off those bad habits...well, it won't be easy until it is. The more you do something, the easier it gets. Take full responsibility for your life choices and the habits you have in place.

2. Develop a Morning Routine

Morning routines can encompass a lot of different things. I like to start my morning routine with my Morning Upgrade cards. This is a staple of my morning routine. Depending on the season of life I'm in, I like to add in things to what I do. For example, right now I'm reading a chapter of a book after I do the cards.

I think that reading daily is essential to being a leader...and all of us are leaders of ourselves. Even if you only have time to read 3 pages per day, it will introduce you to new ways of thinking and will build your momentum.

3. Take Time to Journal

Journaling on a regular basis is a great way to advance on your personal development journey. To start, I want you to take an hour and journal on what it looks like to be your own hero. Here are a few prompts to help you:

What does it mean for me to be my own hero?

What does the hero version of myself look like?How does that person compare to who I am right now? What am I doing (or not doing) that will help me close the gap between who I am and who I can become? It will really help you to get crystal clear on what the hero version of you looks like because it will give you a target to aim for.

4. Exercise Every Day and Eat Well

Exercising is important for your health, but it also helps you to feel happier and calmer because of the endorphins it releases. When you exercise, you can easily do habit stacking where you listen to a podcast or Audible to educate yourself. Or, you can use it as a time of silence to connect with your environment and unplug i.e. going for a walk outside...so relaxing!

Also, eating well is essential to feeling good and having the energy to tackle the day. I'm not saying you can't ever splurge, but do what you can to focus on eating right 90% of the time.

5.Look for Ways to Get Out of Your Comfort Zone

What does it look like for you to get out of your comfort zone? Maybe it's speaking to strangers or doing things you don't know how to do. Don't let the fear of something keep you from trying new things. You'll likely make mistakes, but that's ok.

Case in point:

When I wrote my book, I read it over after getting it printed and found some mistakes I made and other things I wanted to change. Sigh. Not only did I make these errors, but about a month after I started selling the book, I realized I didn't have artwork on the spine of the book. Sigh again, lol.

What I want you to take away from this point is that you don't have to do something perfectly. Instead, be willing to try new things and to make mistakes. Focus on learning and doing instead of getting everything correct right from the start.

6.Expect Challenges and Be Ok With Them

Life is a constant state of change and filled with obstacles you have to overcome. Expect that you will have challenges you have to deal with and be ok with it. How you react to the problems is within your control, not the problem itself. Go into life knowing that problems will happen...and when they do, they'll suck less because you expected them.

12

Achieve your goals

If you want to succeed at anything in life, you need to know how to achieve your goals.Goals give us a sense of direction and focus. Without them, we would be wandering aimlessly. If you don't have a clear understanding of where you want to go, then how do you expect to ever get there?

We all want to achieve something great in our lives, yet many of us don't know what it takes in order to reach our desired outcome. The trick is knowing how to move from wanting something to actually following through and making it happen. Setting goals is a good start, but it's not enough. If you don't have a plan in place for execution, you will fail.

When you look at the statistics for failure to achieve goals, the numbers are shocking. According to research by the University of Scranton, 92 percent of people that set New Year's goals never actually achieve them. Failure to achieve your goals can leave you feeling disappointed and depressed. The result? People give up.

If you want to be one of the 8% who succeeds, you need to know how to achieve your goals. Don't expect to say, "This is what I want" and have it magically come true. If you are serious about goal-setting, you need to understand that it is a process that takes time, commitment, hard work, and patience.

In the words of Brad Burden, "Winners must have two things; definite goals and a burning desire to achieve them." Are you ready to learn what it takes to be a winner and achieve your goals?

How will you achieve your goals?

Before you can even think about setting or achieving your goals, you need to understand the difference between results-oriented and process-oriented goals.

Results-oriented goals are focused towards a specific result. Ultimately, a result is what you are striving for. However, if you only concern yourself with the final outcome, you are making a big mistake. Don't forget about the process that it takes in order to achieve your goals.

Process-oriented goals are small milestones that remind you that you are going in the right direction. Think of process-based goals as habits. Once you have mastered habits, then you can turn your focus towards the results that those habits are supposed to create.

I am a firm believer that, if you want to achieve your goals, you need to focus on and enjoy the process. This is my goal-setting strategy for success. In the words of Eric Thomas, "Fall in love with the process and the results will come."

1. Make A Commitment

If you want to achieve your goals, you need to first make a commitment to yourself. Look at the current state of your life and ask yourself, "What is the consequence of NOT achieving my goals?"

If there is something that is holding you back, go inward and figure out what it is. If you are waiting for the perfect moment to commit to achieving your goals, you are going to be waiting a long time.

As William James once proclaimed, "To change one's life: Start immediately. Do it flamboyantly. No exceptions." Are you ready to go all in?

2. Aim High, But Start Small

When it comes to setting goals, it's important to aim high. Big goals are awesome, in that they inspire us to take action. However, I see a lot of people that set big goals that are too grandiose. As a result, they never get achieved.I'm a big believer that, when it comes to setting goals, you need to start small. Sometimes when we look at the big picture, our goals can feel unattainable, which is why we need to celebrate the small milestones that we make on a daily basis.

This idea is supported by Harvard researcher Teresa Amabile who points out that the single most powerful workplace motivator is small, daily progress which has the power to ignite joy and engagement in people.I probably have over 50 plus goals. The reason why I never get overwhelmed with the number of goals that I have is that I don't focus on all of my goals at once. I hone in on 1-2 projects at a time, and then as I grow, I celebrate my wins and slowly start taking on more goals.

3. Determine Your Level of Desire and Belief

Whenever you set a goal, your intention is always to change something. In order to achieve your goals, you need to have a deep-seeded desire to change throughout the entire goal-setting process.

When you set a goal, ask yourself, "On a scale from 1-10, what is my level of desire to achieve this goal?" If your desire is a 2, then obviously you won't have the momentum that you need in order to achieve your goals. You want your desire to be in the range of 7-10.

Here's the kicker. Desire isn't enough. You also need to possess an unwavering belief in your ability to achieve your goals, which is why you also need to ask yourself, "On a scale from 1-10, what is my level of belief that I can achieve this goal?"

If you have a desire to make $10 million dollars this year, but your belief is at a 1, you are setting yourself up for failure. This is where a lot of people get stuck. They set goals, but because their desire and/or belief is not in alignment with the goal that they want to achieve, they fail.

The result? They drop into avoidance mode and forget about their goals altogether.

When you find the sweet spot, where your desire and your belief are in full alignment with your goals, you are setting yourself up for success. This goal-setting formula is what has allowed me to achieve my goals and take my life to the next level.

4. Drop Bad Habits

Achieving your goals is not so much about mastering the art of goal-setting, as it is about dropping the bad habits that are holding you back from success.

Our brains are hard-wired to prefer routine over something new, so when we are trying to kick a bad habit there is always some resistance. The result is that it inhibits our ability to make progress. Bring yourself back to "here and now" and stop thinking too far into the future.

Take the focus away from the goal itself and how you are going to get there and learn to fall in love with the process of who you want to become.

In the words of Leo Tolstoy, "Remember then: there is only one time that is important — Now. It is the most important time because it is the only time when we have any power."

5. Be Consistent

To be consistent means that you commit to taking action over the long-term. It means that you are willing to go all-in and fully dedicate yourself to achieving your goals. This is what a master does. They don't get distracted by shiny objects. Rather, they are hyper-focused. Nothing stands in their way of success. If they can't find a way, they make a way.

Consistency comes down to repetition. If you want to master your life, you need to commit to repeating the same habits and rituals over and over again. One of the best ways to trick your brain into helping you achieve your goals is by consistently engaging in the habit that you want to adopt.

By working towards your goal, every day, it will be easier for your brain to convert that behavior into a habit. This is why I am such a big fan of morning rituals, as they help you make progress towards your goals by conditioning your mindset for success every day.

6. Don't Give Up!

The people who always succeed in achieving their goals are the ones who never give up. If you are expecting an easy, breezy ride on the road to success, keep dreaming. Anything of value requires hard work and persistence.

Your ability to overcome the challenges that you face along the way makes accomplishing your goals all that sweeter.

The fact that you have read this entire blog shows me that you are the type of person that is committed to doing whatever it takes to achieve your goals. Someone once said, "Giving up on your goal because of one setback is like slashing your other 3 tires because you got one flat." Follow your dreams and don't ever give up.

7. Set SMART goals

If you've done your reading about goal-setting, you've probably already heard about the SMART method. This acronym stands for goals that are:

Specific: What are you trying to accomplish? What actions will you take?

Measurable: How will you know you succeeded?Time-bound: What is your deadline?Both your career and personal goals should follow this method. It will help you set realistic expectations for what you can achieve, saving you from disappointment and discouragement if you miss your mark.

And while failure is a great teacher, nothing kills motivation faster than feeling like you failed.

8.Track your progress

Once you get into the flow of setting and achieving goals, it's easy to lose track of how far you've come. Create a system or download an app to view your progress regularly. This will keep you motivated as you progress. A visual representation like a checklist or a fundraising thermometer works well.

One day a son came to his father for an advice:
– Dad, I can't do this anymore, – he said, – those lessons only exhaust me, and the result doesn't change. It must be not destined for me to play football and my dream will never come true.
The father looked at his son with loving eyes and said:
– You know son, every person in life has a dream, a goal of his life. They are the ones that make us do what we are doing, because it's what we should do. We have to fight for what we believe in, what we feel. In other case, you will simply brake. Once – and for all.

The easiest way is to quit everything and not go until the end, because the path is difficult and we are not used to inconveniences. We want everything to be easy and at once. But the wishes are fleeting! This is how our dream dies, and the goal becomes unreachable.

Gradually, life becomes a routine without depth and meaning. Then one day, we try to forget and start everything from the beginning, we wait for a new day to make our life different. But new obstacles come in our way, and we stop again. We become full of despair and anger for our own helplessness.

But you only need to remember one thing: never give up, fight, battle. It doesn't matter that you have lost one battle and even dozens of battles. Life goes on! Your biggest enemies are hiding in you – laziness, fear, doubt, indecision. Be a warrior of your dream, a knight of your goal and a soldier of your wishes!

13

Stories

1.power of silence

Once a farmer lost his precious watch while working in his barn. It may have appeared as an ordinary watch to others but held a deep sentimental value.After searching high and low among the hay for a long time, the old farmer got exhausted. However, the tired farmer did not want to give up the search for his watch and requested a group of children playing outside the barn to help. He promised an attractive reward for the person who could find his beloved watch.After hearing about the reward, the children hurried inside the barn and went around the entire stack of hay to find the watch. After a long time of looking for a watch in the hay, some of the children got tired and gave up. The number of children looking for the watch slowly decreased, and only a few tired children were left. The farmer gave up his hope of finding his watch and called off the search.

When the farmer was closing the door, a little boy came up to him and requested the farmer give him another chance. The farmer did not want to miss any chance of finding the watch, so he left the little boy in the barn.

After a little while, the little boy came out with the watch in his hand. The farmer was happily surprised and asked how the boy succeeded in getting the watch while everyone, including him, had failed.The boy replied, "I just sat there trying to listen to the watch's ticking. In silence, it was much easier to listen to it and direct the search toward the sound."The farmer was delighted to get the watch and rewarded the little boy as promised.A peaceful mind can think better than a worked-up mind. So once in a while, allow a few minutes of silence to your mind. Sometimes all you need to do is relax and listen.

2.I KNOW WHY THE CAGED BIRD SINGS BY MAYA ANGELOU

Maya Angelou recounts her traumatic childhood growing up in the American South in the turbulent 1930's. At the age of three, her parent's divorce divided her family. She and her brother Bailey were sent to live with her grandmother in rural Stamps, Arkansas. Her grandmother, a shopkeeper, otherwise known as 'Momma,' became a strong maternal figure to Maya. Momma became a center of stability in her formative years. Maya fights her sense of abandonment and self-worth in a community beset by poverty, rampant violence, and racial discrimination.

Maya and Bailey's lives were upended once more when their father returned them to their mother in St Louis, Missouri. Her mother lives a wild life at the gambling parlors. She is an indifferent parent, negligent and self-obsessed. Maya bares her soul about her childhood sexual abuse at the hands of her mother's boyfriend.She explores her childhood trauma poetically and poignantly, where the murder of her abuser compounds her trauma from her rape. Maya's guilt and pain result in her withdrawing into a silence that only Bailey can penetrate.

When Maya is returned to Momma, she learns to speak her heart again when Mrs. Bertha Flowers introduces her to literature. Through reading aloud, Maya begins to learn how to use language to create and heal. This discovery sets her on the path of becoming one of the world's most treasured poets.

The book also explores identity issues when faced with dehumanizing racism, which Maya experienced in her formative years. In the heart of the South, she faced racism at its worst and expresses its effects through the eyes of her younger self.

The abject poverty of the community where Maya lived made her success even more unlikely and inspiring. Ultimately, the book is a testament to the power of love and the human spirit to overcome even the most traumatic childhoods.

3.MAN'S SEARCH FOR MEANING VICTOR E FRANKL

Austrian-born neurologist and psychiatrist Victor E Frankl recounts his experience of being imprisoned in a Nazi concentration camp called Theresienstadt. There, he lost his father, mother, and wife to the holocaust horrors of the Nazi regime.

He uses his experiences and the experiences of others in this state of horror and oppression to suggest a new means of finding value in the world through each moment. He recounts how he used his suffering and experiences in the war camps to deepen himself as a person and grow spiritually.

Essentially the work is a testament to the human will that ultimately decides whether to allow circumstances to dictate their destiny. The experiences that he recounts underlie his concept of logotherapy and explore the possibility of the human mind to transcend trauma and embrace meaning.

Ultimately each man must search for his meaning in his work, love, and suffering, according to Frankl. His story is ultimately one of empowerment in that despite the most deplorable of circumstances, if a man can find meaning, he can survive anything.

Bill Gates Success Story: The Man who brought OS Systems
Being passionate about a thing and following that until you achieve it leads you to the path of success. So is the story of the now Philanthropist Bill gates. His story is not from the poor to rich, he had a wealthy family, his father being an

attorney and mother being a school teacher, but the amount of work he had put in to create what he is today regardless of the background he had, made him stand out from the rest.

Bill Gates Success Story - EARLY DAYS
It all started in school at the age of 13, where he got a computer system from a general electronic company, offered by the school, on which he started his success journey by building the first software of his life. Since then, he never stopped, he built many more with his schoolmate Paul Allen. Together they wrote a payroll program, software helping in school schedule management, traffic optimizing software, and one more which help them earn profit.

Gates was very intelligent in academics, especially in Maths, and appeared for SAT after completing school and cleared it with flying colors. This led to his entry into the famous Harvard institute, but because of his interest in computers and programming he couldn't abide by the long, stressful, "doing the same thing everyday" days in Harvard as he couldn't do what he really wanted to, so he decided to take a break from Harvard (which he eventually left) and work will Paul Allen in the field of developing software.

Both worked in a small space and created many software. While working on a programming language, Allen came across an article that read about an Altair created by MITS. Gates found this opportunity interesting and contacted the MITS and told them about BASIC, the programming language they were working on. Soon they demonstrated the program to the company and it sold the program as Altair-BASIC.

Bill Gates Company - Micro-Soft (with a hyphen) This invention motivated them to open a company of their own, they named it as Micro-Soft. The company suffered losses initially as they were using pirated systems but soon, they had been contacted by a company called IBM, which asked them to make an operating system for the launch of their first manufactured computer. Initially, Gates offered them another company for developing the system but ended up making an OS himself, knocking out the company he offered IBM.

The OS which Gates developed was not an original but an innovation of an existing OS, he named his OS, MS-DOS. This system was then licensed by many other companies. Being satisfied with the product given by Gates after a few years, IBM approached them again and asked them to develop another operating system, Gates took the challenge and this made him develop yet another operating system, OS2.

After a few years, Gates and Paul Allen built a software named Windows, a collection of operating systems, which overshadowed the operating systems they had made before. This led to a partition between IBM and Micro-Soft because of the competition in the market. After the launch of Windows, many other versions were also released, one of which merged the OS and Windows both in one.

This much development was not enough for the now entrepreneur Gates, his hunger was still not satisfied. He worked on various other software and this led him to develop one of the famous programs Microsoft offices. Today no computer is sold without this program. It has become a necessity for every individual either related to the computer field or not.

Apart from the programs which are described, many more were developed from the intelligent brains of Mr. Gate. During the path of their success, Allen was diagnosed with a disease, after the recovery, he decides to part ways with Gates and moves on in life to peruse various Business ventures.

Gates went ahead with creating the now named Microsoft (without the hyphen) and today is the principal founder of the company. He had been assigned the position of CEO, he stepped back from the position and now is the chairman of the company and an advisor to the new CEO.

Gates didn't only earn money in his life but the billionaire who he is today shared his worth with people in need. As mentioned, he stepped down from the CEO position, he invested his time in the William Foundations, which is now working under Gates and his wife. They worked towards social problems like poverty, inequality, hygiene, healthcare, and many more. Gates representing the IT field invested some amount for the betterment of the field.

Top Bill Gates Habits for Success
Getting successful on your own is not easy. For Gates also it wasn't. But he followed few habits which led him to the path of success.

HARDWORK-
He donated most of his time to his passion and worked on his product's improvement. He was very dedicated to what he was doing and knew exactly what he was doing.
GOOD COMPANY-

one spoilt Apple can spoil the whole basket of apples, i.e., the company you are with, has a huge impact on your entire life be it friends, family, relatives, etc. Staying around motivating people helped Gates develop confidence in what he was doing and with some help he achieved what he wanted.

COMPETITION –

having competition motivates a person to get better in the field they are in. Being in an IT field Gates had to face a lot of competition, the pressure which developed because of the competition made him think differently.

DESIRE–

The burning desire to be different helped Gates develop innovative software from the existing versions which help him increase the market value of his products.

DIFFERENT THINKING –

Gates thought out of the box and didn't do what everyone else was doing. He did what he wanted to do and did it in a way he wanted to do it.

Final Words on Legend – Bill Gates Success Story Learning from the motivating Bill Gates who now gives speeches in various institutions, including Harvard, which he left, Gates has achieved everything he has dreamed of, he is today an idol for many and has many followers who follow his principles of success. Continuing to inspire many today Gates is living a very fulfilling life many dreams of getting.

Another of Bill Gates' success lessons is to learn that life is not fair. No matter how hard you work in life, there will always be times where things don't go your way, perhaps through no fault of your own. Things that you cannot control. You will get knocked down, but you need to be able to stand up. Life isn't fair.